Sports Illustrated KIDS

GAME DAY

VIP PASS

TO A
PRO BASEBALL
GAME DAY

FROM THE LOCKER ROOM TO THE PRESS BOX
[AND EVERYTHING IN BETWEEN]

by Clay Latimer

Consultant:
Joe Schmit
Sports Director, KSTP-TV
St. Paul, Minnesota

CAPSTONE PRESS
a capstone imprint

P9-DFB-919

Sports Illustrated KIDS Game Day is published by Capstone Press,
151 Good Counsel Drive, P.O. Box 669, Mankato, Minnesota 56002.
www.capstonepub.com

Books published by Capstone Press are manufactured with paper
containing at least 10 percent post-consumer waste.

Library of Congress Cataloging-in-Publication Data
Latimer, Clay, 1952–
    VIP pass to a pro baseball game day: from the locker room to the press box
    (and everything in between) / by Clay Latimer.
    p. cm.—(Sports Illustrated KIDS. Game day.)
    Includes bibliographical references and index.
    Summary: "Describes various activities and people who work behind the
scenes during a Major League Baseball game"—Provided by publisher.
    ISBN 978-1-4296-5462-3 (library binding)
    ISBN 978-1-4296-6283-3 (paperback)
1. Baseball—Juvenile literature. 2. Major League Baseball
(Organization)—Juvenile literature. I. Title.
GV867.5.L38 2011
796.357—dc22   2010032208

Editorial Credits

Aaron Sautter, editor; Ted Williams, designer; Eric Gohl,
    media researcher; Eric Manske, production specialist

Photo Credits

Getty Images Inc./Christian Petersen, 24; MLB Photos/Michael Zagaris, 6;
    MLB Photos/Rich Pilling, 20; Scott Olson, 29
Shutterstock/David Lee, background (baseball field)
Sports Illustrated/Al Tielemans, cover, 4, 17; Bob Rosato, 11, 23; Damian
    Strohmeyer, 12, 13, 27; David E. Klutho, 9, 16; Heinz Kluetmeier, 7, 28;
    John Biever, 26; John Iacono, 15; Robert Beck, 18

Design Elements

Shutterstock/bioraven; Daniela Illing; Iwona Grodzka;
    Marilyn Volan; Zavodskov Anatoliy Nikolaevich

Printed in the United States of America in Stevens Point, Wisconsin.
092010   005934WZS11

TABLE OF CONTENTS

"Play ball!" Baseball fans love hearing those wonderful words. A Major League Baseball (MLB) game offers fans plenty of entertainment and interesting action. But a lot happens behind the scenes that the fans never see. Behind every stolen base there's a coach that flashes signals to the players. Every relief pitcher has a great **bullpen** story. During the game, coaches discuss strategy in the **dugouts**. Grounds crews continually work to keep the field in tip-top shape.

To understand the big picture you have to look beyond the field. How do teams travel? What do they do before the first pitch? How do umpires prepare for a game? There's much more to baseball than just the game on the field.

bullpen—an area where relief pitchers warm up during a game

dugout—a sunken shelter where players and coaches sit during a game

SPORTS FACT

The first baseball game played under official rules took place on June 19, 1846. The New York Nine pummeled the New York Knickerbockers, 23-1.

TAKING OFF

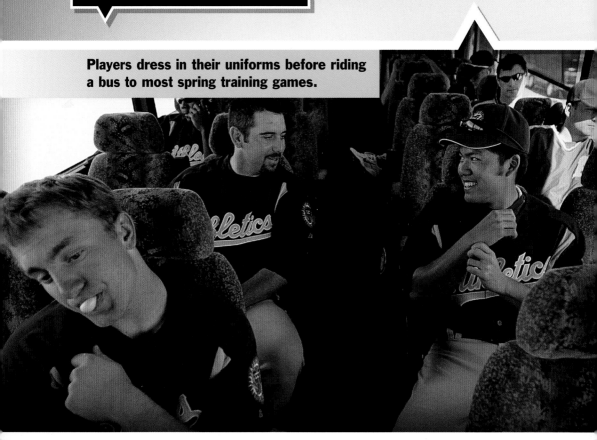

Players dress in their uniforms before riding a bus to most spring training games.

The last game of a three-game series is over. The players board a cushy bus, which will take them to a nearby city. They're in the middle of a long road trip. They sink back into their seats, and gradually begin to unwind. Traveling between games can be an exhausting grind.

Major-league teams typically travel on private chartered jets. But sometimes they take a bus to a nearby city. No matter how they travel, the players are treated like kings. They eat fine food and have plenty of room to stretch their tired bodies. A few sleep while others watch movies, listen to music, or talk baseball. Meanwhile, coaches study reports on the next opponent.

Eventually the team arrives at a fancy hotel. The players head to their rooms to get comfortable and settle in. It will be their home for the next several days.

▮ SPRING TRAINING

Every spring, baseball teams head to Arizona or Florida to prepare for another season. Spring training begins in February and lasts nearly two months. For the regulars, spring training is about getting in shape to get through a long season. For the younger players, it's a time to try to get a starting job.

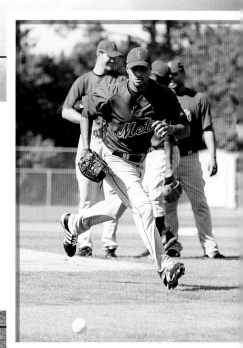

HOME AWAY FROM HOME

Players spend up to eight hours at the stadium every game day. But only about three or four hours are spent playing ball. The rest of the time is spent warming up or hanging out in the clubhouse.

On game day players first go to the clubhouse to change into their practice uniforms. A few players might get a massage in the trainer's room. The others head to the field to stretch and take batting practice. Then they return to the clubhouse to change into their official game uniforms.

◼ WILD BELIEFS

When it comes to superstitions and weird habits, it's hard to top baseball players. Former New York Mets pitcher Turk Wendell brushed his teeth and chewed licorice between every inning. Former pitcher Mark "The Bird" Fidrych talked to both himself and the ball. Jose Rijo applied snake oil to his pitching arm to keep it loose.

The clubhouse is the players' home away from home. They can play cards, talk baseball, watch TV, and eat their meals there. Players stay well fed at the clubhouse. They enjoy a full buffet table loaded with pasta, ribs, and other fine foods.

Soon it's time to take the field. The players file out of the clubhouse with their bats and gloves. They're ready to go to work.

The team clubhouse is a relaxing place for players when they're not on the field.

GETTING LOOSE

Smack! A baseball goes flying. Crack! There goes another one—right out of the park. Batting practice is the time for hitters to take practice swings. It's part of the pre-game ritual. Players hustle in and out to take their turn in the **batting cage**. When the players have each taken their turn, they gather up loose balls in front of the batting cage. Soon a coach from the other team rolls a cart full of balls toward the mound. It's his team's turn for batting practice.

batting cage—a screen placed behind home plate to catch balls during batting practice

SPORTS FACT

Players didn't wear gloves in baseball's early years. In 1870 Doug Allison of the Cincinnati Red Stockings was the first pro player to wear a glove.

Players warm up with stretching exercises before each game.

Pre-game routines include more than just batting practice. Before the game, players emerge from the dugout to stretch and jog along the base lines. Then they head onto the field to loosen up and practice their fielding skills. Meanwhile, the starting pitchers warm up their pitching arms in the bullpen.

POLISHING THE DIAMOND

Groundskeepers work hard to keep the field in perfect condition. The head groundskeeper arrives at the park before dawn to inspect the field for any problems. Less than an hour before the game, grounds crew members get busy. They break down the batting cage. They water down the infield, making sure they don't create puddles. They rake the dirt around home plate. They also paint the plate so it's bright white.

Grounds crews rake and smooth out the infield dirt between innings.

Grounds crews repaint the ballfield lines for each game.

Grounds crews keep working even after the first pitch. After the third inning, they rake the infield and smooth out the dirt. They repeat this task again after the fifth and seventh innings.

Their jobs aren't done even when the game is over. Crew members work for about an hour after the game is finished. They repair gouges in the batters' boxes made by players' shoe spikes. They also repaint the baselines and water the outfield. They'll be back at least 12 hours before the next game—ready to put in another day of work on the field.

GETTING OUT OF THE PEN

The bullpen door swings open and a murmur flows through the stadium. The team's closer makes his way to the pitcher's mound. He's determined to save the game.

Bullpens are located behind the outfield fence. The players and pitching coach all sit in comfy seats during the game. There's plenty of room to stretch and throw warm-up pitches. To pass time, some pitchers study the hitters on the other team. The atmosphere is relaxed and casual. But then the phone rings. The team's manager is calling. It's time to bring in a reliever. The mood is suddenly serious. It's time to go to work and try to win the game.

Bullpen roles are clearly defined. Long men, set-up pitchers, and closers all pitch only in certain innings. Long men usually pitch in the 6th and 7th innings. Set-up men pitch in the 7th and 8th innings. Closers go to work in the 9th to finish out the game. Each pitcher knows his role, and they work together to go for the win.

Relief pitchers stay loose in the bullpen until they are needed in the game.

■ GRAND ENTRANCES

Many relief pitchers like to make a grand entrance when they enter the game. When the bullpen gate opens, booming entrance music floods the ballpark. New York Yankees closer Mariano Rivera walks to the mound while Metallica's *Enter Sandman* rocks the stadium. Milwaukee closer Trevor Hoffman enters the game to the sound of AC/DC's *Hells Bells*.

BUNKER MENTALITY

Players focus on the game action while in the team dugout.

Baseball fields have perfectly trimmed grass and raked infield dirt. Clubhouses are relaxing places with wide-screen TVs and freshly cooked meals. But there's nothing fancy about a dugout.

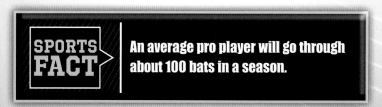

SPORTS FACT An average pro player will go through about 100 bats in a season.

During a game, players can come and go through a dugout's back exit. Some players might head to a video room to study their last at-bats. Others go to the trainer's room to receive treatments for injuries. Inside the dugout, players crack jokes and spit sunflower seeds while waiting for their turn at bat.

A dugout is also a team's workroom. As the game proceeds, players and coaches watch for the opponent's weaknesses. They look for ways to strengthen their own game plan too. By studying pitching charts and other statistics, they hope to find an advantage to win.

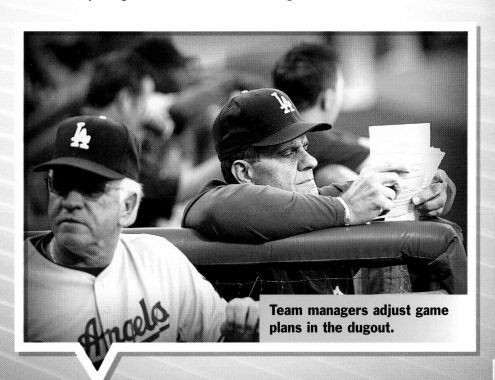

Team managers adjust game plans in the dugout.

LAW AND ORDER

In a small dressing room, an umpire rubs some baseballs to make them less slippery. Then he puts on his chest protector. It's an hour before the first pitch, but the pressure is building.

Umpires may have the hardest job in baseball. During the season they have little time to spend with their families. At the games, fans boo them, players question them, and managers yell at them.

Players sometimes strongly disagree with the umpire's calls at the plate.

On a typical game day, a four-man officiating crew meets for breakfast. Then they go for a run or work out in a gym. They arrive at the stadium hours before the game. They change into their uniforms, and then head to the field to review lineups with team managers and make sure everything is in order.

During the game, the umpire calls balls and strikes at the plate. His crew makes sure runners touch all the bases. And if a player or coach loses his temper, it's the umpire's job to eject the troublemaker from the game.

After the game, the officiating crew discusses any plays they feel need to be reviewed. Then it's time to take a shower, grab a bite to eat, and head back to the hotel. Officials repeat this routine 140 to 150 times during the season. They get only a few days off each season.

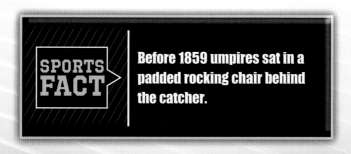

SPORTS FACT

Before 1859 umpires sat in a padded rocking chair behind the catcher.

TELLING THE STORY

Reporters watch the game and take notes from press boxes high above the field.

The first pitch is just minutes away. High up in the press box, reporters are going to work. The radio play-by-play man settles in to call the game. Sports writers flip open their laptop computers. A TV reporter watches as the players warm up on the field. Every baseball game has a small army of **journalists** and broadcasters working hard to keep the fans informed.

journalist—someone who writes news stories

A reporter's day begins hours before the game begins. At the clubhouse, reporters spend time talking to players and coaches. Or they simply roam around looking for a good story. Before the game, team managers hold meetings with the press. It's a chance for reporters to ask questions and learn which players might be out of the game. After the meeting, reporters and broadcasters head back to the press box.

During the game, one reporter keeps notes and writes blog entries for her paper's Web site. When the game is over, another reporter hurries to the clubhouse to interview the manager and a few players. He wants to get more details before writing a story for the paper's late edition.

The radio play-by-play announcers watch the game from a small booth. They describe the action on the field for people listening at home. A small TV monitor sits nearby to give them a closer view of replays and close calls. During pauses in the action, they entertain listeners with stories and little-known facts about the teams.

CALLING THE SHOTS

They work in the bullpen and in the dugout. They stand next to first and third base. They teach the players and listen to their problems. They're the coaches—the men who help the players perform at their very best.

The head coach is called the team manager. The manager makes sure the team is ready for each game. He works with the assistant coaches to figure out batting orders and a game plan for each opponent. During the game, he decides when to change pitchers, when to try a sacrifice **bunt**, and when to send in a **pinch hitter**.

bunt—to tap the ball very gently so it rolls into the infield close to home plate

pinch hitter—a substitute who bats for a teammate

The bench coach is usually second in command. His main job is to help the team manager run the team. It's usually the bench coach who steps in if the manager misses a game or gets ejected. The bench coach also works with players to improve their skills and supervises things like base running.

Coaches direct players as they run around the bases after a hit.

Coaches use secret signs to tell pitchers
and hitters what to do during the game.

Third-base coaches use secret signs during games. The signs tell players when to bunt, let a pitch go, or take a swing. To call a secret play, a coach may touch his ear, nose, leg, arm, or belt. Most of the moves are decoys. But one of them is an indicator. It tells the players that the next signal is the one that matters. Third-base coaches also work to direct traffic on the field. Depending on the play, they signal runners to stop or head for home.

Pitching coaches work with pitchers to improve their delivery. They also teach pitchers how to sharpen their mental focus. Hitting coaches show hitters how to refine their swing. Position coaches help players sharpen their game skills at the plate, in the field, and on the pitching mound.

SPORTS FACT

The Boston Red Sox go through 120 to 140 baseballs for each home game. That's nearly 12,000 balls each season!

ENJOYING THE SHOW

The stadium gates open and fans stream in for the game. The smell of delicious foods fills the air. Kids rush to try to get their favorite players' autographs. For die-hard fans, there's nothing better than the sights, sounds, and smells of a baseball park.

Fans enjoy getting autographs from their favorite players.

With its numerous traditions, baseball is considered America's national pastime. Fans love to eat hot dogs, peanuts, popcorn, and other tasty foods at the game. Mascots roam the stands to entertain the fans. One of the oldest traditions is the seventh-inning stretch. Fans stand and stretch their legs while singing the traditional baseball song *Take Me Out to the Ball Game*.

During the game, the scoreboard might show crowd shots or clips of the home team's greatest moments. Fans might even cheer for their favorite mascot to win a race during a break in the action. A production crew creates all of this fun in the control room. They spend hours preparing for each game to make sure the fans have a good time.

■ MASCOT MISCHIEF

The Phillie Phanatic is a fan favorite at Philadelphia Phillies home games. The big, green, birdlike character is well known for his crazy antics. He often eats fans' popcorn or steals their ice cream. He has fun patting bald people on the head or poking food vendors. Wherever he goes, people are sure to be laughing.

HEADING FOR HOME

Players often congratulate each other after winning games.

Another day at the ballpark draws to a close. Food sellers shut down their stands. Radio announcers pack up their gear. Umpires peel off their uniforms and change into their regular clothes.

In one clubhouse, players hastily shower and dress. They just won the game. But they don't have time to celebrate. They have a plane to catch. The team is going on a road trip. Meanwhile in the other clubhouse, the coaches gather in a small office to discuss possible lineup changes. They just lost their fifth straight game, and they need to figure out a way to stop the losing streak.

Outside the stadium, a long line of cars inches out of the parking lot. The fans are headed home after a fun day at the ballpark. Some of the cars carry the people who worked behind the scenes at the game. They've put in a full day to make the game entertaining for the fans. Tomorrow they'll return for another game and another day of fun.

Crowds of fans enjoy hanging out near the stadium when the home team wins a big game.

GLOSSARY

batting cage (BAT-ing KAYJ)—a movable screen placed behind home plate to catch balls during batting practice

bullpen (BUL-pen)—an area where relief pitchers warm up during a game

bunt (BUHNT)—to tap the ball very gently so it rolls into the infield close to home plate

dugout (DUHG-out)—one of two sunken shelters on either side of the field where players and coaches sit during a game

journalist (JUR-nuh-list)—someone who collects information and writes news stories for newspapers, magazines, TV, or radio

mascot (MASS-kot)—an animal, person, or thing that represents a team

pinch hitter (PINCH HIT-ur)—a substitute who bats for a teammate, often at a critical moment in the game

press box (PRESS BOKS)—a section at a stadium where reporters and journalists sit to watch the game

READ MORE

Berman, Len. *The 25 Greatest Baseball Players of All Time.* Naperville, Ill.: Sourcebooks, 2010.

Buckley, James Jr. *The Child's World Encyclopedia of Baseball.* Mankato, Minn.: Child's World, 2009.

Jacobs, Greg. *The Everything Kids' Baseball Book: Today's Superstars, Great Teams, Legends—and Tips on Playing Like a Pro!* Everything Kids Series. Avon, Mass.: Adams Media, 2006.

INTERNET SITES

FactHound offers a safe, fun way to find Internet sites related to this book. All of the sites on FactHound have been researched by our staff.

Here's all you do:

Visit *www.facthound.com*

Type in this code: 9781429654623

Check out projects, games and lots more at
www.capstonekids.com

INDEX